Contents

- 2 CD-ROMs
- 3 Multimedia presentations
- 4 Adding pictures
- 5 Digital photos and video clips
- 6 Animation
- 7 Adding sound
- 8 Making sound clips
- 9 Super stories
- 10 The slide show
- 11 Making a web page
- 12 Linking pages
- 13 Web favourites
- 14 Organising a Favourites list
- 15 Internet fun
- 16 Surfing
- 17 Safety
- 18 Diagrams and charts
- 19 Word Art
- 20 Tables
- 21 Making a booklet
- 22 Shop survey
- 23 SUM and AutoSum
- 24 Copying formulas
- 25 Changing variables
- 26 Spreadsheet modelling
- 27 Graphs
- 28 Loops and Processes
- 29 How does it work?
- 30 Fun with Paint
- 31 Making movies
- 32 Answers

AGES 10–11
KEY STAGE 2

CD-ROMs

Multimedia uses words, pictures and sound together. A good example of multimedia is a CD-ROM encyclopedia.

Look at this page from a CD-ROM. As well as information, there are buttons or shortcuts that link it to other pages. Most CD-ROMs place their **Option**, **Search**, **Help** and **Home** buttons in the same place on every page.

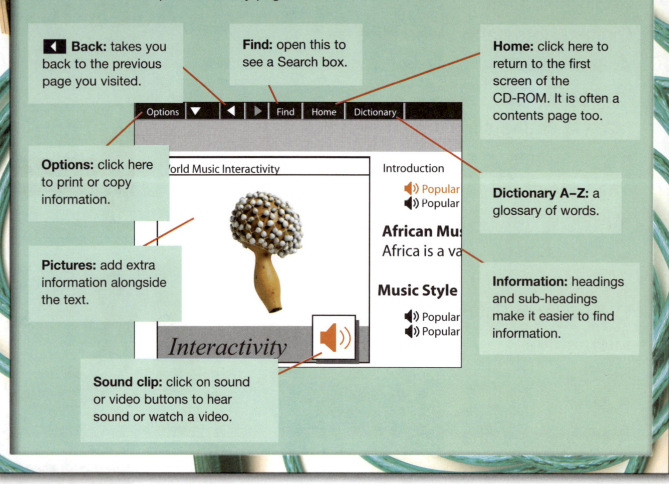

I **Open a CD-ROM encyclopedia.**

Open a **Search box** and type: music.

Click **Search**.

Look at some pages that the **Search engine** has found.

Find a page with a sound clip. What was it? _____

Find a page with a video clip. What was it? _____

II **Browse through pages of a CD-ROM encyclopedia, then answer these questions.**

a Which things stay the same on each page? Why do you think this is?

_____

b Name two ways that you can find a sound or a video clip. _____

c Why do pages use headings and sub-headings? _____

d Why is a **Home** button useful? _____

Multimedia presentations

Multimedia presentations use words, pictures, sound and animation. Presentation software helps you put these together. A presentation is made up of individual slides.

- Open **PowerPoint**.
- Click **Blank presentation** and left mouse click on a blank slide.
- From the **Insert** menu or the shortcut on the **Drawing** toolbar, click **Text Box** 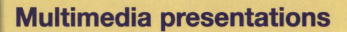.
- Create a text box near the top of the screen for a heading by pressing the left mouse button and dragging the mouse.
- Type the heading: 'My Presentation' in the box.
- Change the size, style and colour of the text and centre it using the formatting buttons on the toolbar.
- To choose a background colour for the slide, open the **Format** menu and choose **Background** or try a **Slide Design**.
- Save the slide in your folder.

It is a good idea to keep the same colour scheme all the way through the slideshow.

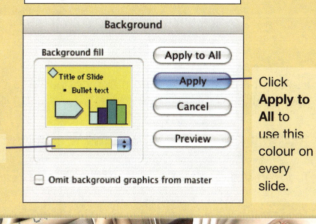

Choose colour.

Click **Apply to All** to use this colour on every slide.

Make the first slide for a slideshow.

Insert a **text box** for a title and add another **text box** for your name.

Experiment with different colours or add a **Slide Design** until you have a colour scheme that works well. Save your work as 'My Presentation'.

Circle the correct phrase to complete these sentences and explain how you would change the colour of a slide.

a You can put a text box
   only at the top of a slide   anywhere on a slide   only at the bottom of a slide.

b A text box is used   to add shapes   to add pictures   to add text.

c A text box   can be any size   is a fixed size   can only be a rectangle shape.

d Slides that are linked together are called presentations or
   viewshows   videos   moving pictures   slideshows.

e How would you change the slide colour?

Adding pictures

Add still and animated pictures to a slide to illustrate the text or for a special effect. An animated picture is one that has some action movement in it. Animated pictures are called **animated gifs**.

The computer has some **animated gifs** stored in the computer's movie clip organiser but you can download others free from the world wide web and save them in your work folder.

To add a still picture to a slide:
- From the **Insert** menu, choose **Picture** and **Clip Art**. Left mouse click on a picture and click on the **Insert** button to add it.

To add an animated gif to a slide:
- From the **Insert** menu, choose **Movies and Sounds** and **Movie from File** or **Movie from Clip Organiser**.
- Left mouse click on a picture to add it. To see the animation before it is added, click the down arrow and choose **Preview**.

To add a saved picture or animated gif from your folder:
- From the **Insert** menu, and choose **Picture**, **From File** or **Movies and Sounds** then **Movie From File**.
- Find the saved file in your folder. Highlight it and left mouse click on **Insert**.

Highlight a picture and drag a corner handle to change its size; use the mouse to drag it to a new position on the slide.

To view the slide, click **SlideShow** 🖵 (bottom left of the screen).

To insert a slide choose 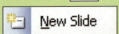 .

To view the whole slideshow, choose **View Show** from the **SlideShow** menu. Press the **Esc** key on the keyboard to stop the slideshow.

I Add still and animated pictures to your slideshow.

Open **PowerPoint** and the file 'My Presentation' (saved on page 3). Add a new blank slide using the shortcut button on the toolbar. Add a **text box** and some text about yourself. Add a picture from the computer's Clip Art gallery and an animated gif.

View the slide and reposition the pictures and text to experiment with different layouts. View the slide each time. Save your work.

II Fill in the gaps in these sentences.

a To add a picture to a slide open the _____, and choose _____, from _____ or from _____.

b To add an animated gif to a slide open the _____ and choose _____, and Movie from _____ or from _____.

c To view a slide click _____. To stop a slideshow press _____.

d Animated gifs are stored in the _____ on the computer's hard drive. Another source of animated gifs is the _____.

Digital photos and video clips

Photos and video clips from digital and video cameras can be added to a slideshow.

To send a photo or video clip to a computer:

- **Install** the camera's software on the computer (this is provided with the camera when you buy it).
- **Take** some photos or a few seconds of video.
- **Connect** the camera to the computer. Most software automatically opens and downloads the pictures or you may need to click **Download**.
- **Save** the pictures in a **Pictures** folder.

To make a new folder:

- Click **Start**, **Documents** and **My Documents**.
- Click **File**, **New** and **Folder**. Give the folder a name.

To add a saved photo or video clip to a slide, use the instructions given on page 4 for inserting a picture or animation from **File**.

Taking digital photos:

- Hold the camera confidently with two hands.
- Place your feet slightly apart so you are well balanced.
- Look through the viewfinder (with some cameras you can look at the small view screen instead).
- Focus on what you are going to take.
- Press the shutter release button as smoothly as possible, keeping the camera steady.

Add some digital photos to your presentation.

Take some photos with a digital camera for your presentation.

Download them into a 'My Pictures' folder.

Open **PowerPoint** and the file 'My Presentation' and add a photo to the first slide.

View the slideshow and save it.

Use the clues to find the missing words:

a You can add this type of photo to a slideshow.   ____ ____ ____ ____ ____ ____ ____

b This means 'to send photos from a digital camera to the computer'.   ____ ____ ____ ____ ____ ____ ____ ____

c Make one of these to store photos and video clips.   ____ ____ ____ ____ ____ ____

d Use this menu to add a saved photo to a slide.   ____ ____ ____ ____ ____ ____

e You need to install this to be able to download photos.   ____ ____ ____ ____ ____ ____ ____ ____

Animation

Animation is a presentation tool that makes words or pictures appear on the slide in different ways. It is one of the most exciting things you can do with presentation software.

- Open **PowerPoint**.
- Add a picture to a slide and highlight it with a left mouse click so you can see the handles around it.
- Open the **Slide Show** menu and choose **Custom Animation**.
- Click on the **Effects** tab, .
- Choose **Entrance** and **Fly In**.
- In the **Direction** box select **From Top** and in the **Speed** box select **Slow**.
- Click **Preview** to watch what happens.
- Click **OK** when you are happy with the action.
- Save the presentation.

You can add effects to text boxes and graphics.

To reorder a sequence of moves, highlight and drag the numbered objects into the order you want them to appear on the screen.

For different sound effects: left mouse click here.

Add a sound effect as the object appears: highlight the object, click the down arrow to see an option box and choose a Sound.

I Add effects to your slideshow.

Open **PowerPoint** and the file 'My Presentation'.

Insert a **New Slide** and add at least one **text box** and two pictures to the slide.

Use **Custom Animation** to try out different **effects** with each **text box** and picture.

Reorder the effects to see which looks best. View the slide each time you make a change.

Add a sound effect to some of the animation but be careful, don't overdo it! A good multimedia slide uses **effects** that go well together.

View both slides as a slideshow: open the **Slide Show** menu and click **View Show**.

II Describe these effects.

a Fly _____

b Spin _____

c Checkerboard _____

d Diamond _____

e How would you delete an effect you didn't want? _____

Adding sound

Another special effect you can add to a slide is a sound clip. A sound clip is different from a sound effect. It is not added to an object and it plays for much longer. The computer has some ready-made sound clips in a sound clip organiser.

To add a sound clip to a slide:

- Open **PowerPoint**.
- From the **Insert** menu, choose **Movies and Sounds** and **Sound from Clip Organiser**. **Search** for a sound in the Sound clip gallery.
- To listen to the sound clip before you add it to the slide, click the down arrow and choose **Preview**.
- Close the **Preview** box and double click on the sound image to add the sound to the slide.

You can choose to play the sound automatically during the slideshow or play it when you click on a **sound button** shown on the slide.

Finally, drag the sound button to reposition it on the slide.

 Make a sound clip presentation.

Open **PowerPoint** and choose **Blank Presentation** and a blank slide.

Create a **text box** with the title: 'My Favourite Sounds'.

Add a sound clip and choose the option to **play** the sound **automatically**.

Insert a **new slide**.

Listen to and add five sound clips to the second slide. Use the option **play on mouse click** for each clip.

Add some Clip Art next to each sound clip. Try to choose a picture that matches the sound or the music. Save the presentation as: 'Sounds' and view the **slide show**.

 All the slides listed here use sound clips. Choose which ones you would set up to play automatically and which you would choose to play on a mouse click. Explain your reasons.

a The sounds of percussion instruments _____

b A multimedia birthday card _____

c An illustrated nursery rhyme for younger children _____

d A page of your favourite sound clips _____

Making sound clips

Make your own sound clips using a microphone and sound recorder software.

- Connect a microphone to the computer. This is often connected to the MIC socket at the back of the computer, but check the microphone's instructions before you start.
- Open the **Sound Recorder** program by clicking **Start, Programs, Accessories, Entertainment** and **Sound Recorder**.
- On the **File** menu, click **New**.
- To begin recording, click **Record** 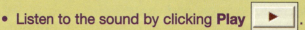.
- To stop recording, click **Stop** .
- Listen to the sound by clicking **Play** 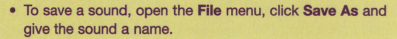.
- To save a sound, open the **File** menu, click **Save As** and give the sound a name.

It is a good idea to save these files in a folder where you can find them easily. Recorded sounds are saved as **.wav** files.

You can add effects to a file or delete any bits of it that you don't want by using the **Effects** or **Edit** menu options.

 Make a PowerPoint slide using your own sound clips.

a Use the **Sound Recorder** and a microphone to record and save three files:
  - some music from a CD
  - an everyday sound such as a clock ticking
  - your voice – remember to speak clearly into the microphone.

  Open the **Sound Recorder**. Click **File** and open the file to play it.

b Play your sounds and try different **effects** using the options in the **effects** menu. If you don't have a microphone, Search yahooligans.yahoo.com for **.wav** files. **Save** a file to your folder by right clicking the mouse and choosing **Save As**. To listen to the file, open the file from the **Sound Recorder** using the **File** menu and click **Play**.

c Design a **PowerPoint** slide using your sound clips.

 Look at the Sound Recorder options and menus and answer these questions.

a What do these buttons do?

   _____   _____

b List three different **effects** that you can create with your sound file. _____

  _____

Super stories

A good slideshow is one that has been carefully planned and organised.

Here is a storyboard for the diary of an evacuee. A storyboard is an outline plan for a story, summarising what happens on each page. This plan helps you organise the slideshow.

1. Title page Picture of diary/book 'Farm sounds'	2. In the city Picture of city 'City sounds'	3. The bombs fall A bombed house 'Siren sound'	4. Plan to evacuate Picture of people in an office 'People in office talking'
5. A train journey Picture of train 'Train sounds'	6. In the country Picture of country 'Country sounds'	7. School and play Picture of children 'Playground sounds'	8. Journey home Picture of train 'Train sounds'

Presentation software has templates. They make it easier to design each slide.

- Open **PowerPoint** and choose **Blank presentation**.
- In the slide options, choose a **Title Slide** and add the title: 'The Diary of an Evacuee'.
- **Insert** a **New Slide** and choose a **Title only** slide.

  Type the page heading: 'In the city'. Continue to add slides and page headings.
- Click **Save As** and use the file name: 'Evacuee Diary'.
- Work on each slide of the diary, adding pictures and sounds and text.

I **Write a storyboard for a slideshow with the title: What did people eat during the war?**

a Design the storyboard to include ideas for pictures and sounds. Number the boxes or draw arrows to show the slide order.

b Create all the slides for your presentation, adding a page heading for each slide. Save your presentation using the file name: 'Food in the War'.

c Work on each slide, adding words, pictures and sounds. Use the formatting tools to change the text and background colour of the slides. Imagine you are making the presentation for your friends at school. The words you use should be suitable for your audience. Remember to save your work regularly.

d Finally add some animation effects. Show your presentation to family and friends – maybe you could show it at school through a data projector!

II **Look at these tabs to the left of the screen.**

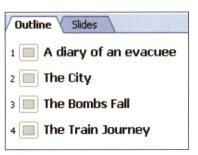

a What happens if you click on **Slides**?

b What happens if you change the text in **Outline**?

c How can these two tools help you plan and organise a slideshow?

The slide show

A slideshow can be set up to run automatically or you can control it using the mouse. To make the slide look more professional, add action buttons to each slide.

- Open **PowerPoint** and from the **File** menu, click **Open**. Open a saved presentation.
- Open the **SlideShow** menu and select **Slide Transition**.

To control the slideshow with the mouse, tick here.

To set the slideshow to run automatically, tick here and choose the number of seconds you want each slide to stay on the screen.

- Click **Apply to All**.

To add **Action Buttons** to a slide:

- Click here.
- When the mouse cursor changes to a cross, press the left button and hold and drag the mouse to draw an arrow in the bottom right corner of the slide.
- Highlight the arrow, open the **Slide Show** menu, **Action Settings** and tick **Hyperlink to** and **Next Slide**.
- Add forward or back arrow buttons to each slide and set the **Action Settings** (which appears on-screen once you have added an action button) for each button: choose **Hyperlink to Next Slide** when going forward and to **Last Slide** when going back.

Click on the forward arrow action button to move to the next slide when viewing the show.

 Practise adding Action buttons.

Open the presentation: 'Food in the War'.

Set up the slide to run on mouse click.

Add forward and back action buttons to each slide.

Run the slideshow using the action buttons to move to the next slide.

 Find these 12 words connected with PowerPoint.

n	s	p	o	n	i	p	s	p
a	n	i	m	a	t	i	o	n
e	o	c	o	l	c	l	u	i
d	e	t	v	v	e	c	n	t
i	d	u	i	i	f	l	d	x
l	i	r	n	e	f	l	y	e
s	v	e	g	w	e	x	e	t

view   animation   sound   text
picture   effect   clip   spin
slide   moving   video   fly

10

Making a web page

Web pages are written in a special language called **html**. To create a website, it is a good idea to use authoring software, but you can make a simple web page using **Microsoft Word**.

- Open **Word**, type some sentences and add a picture from **Clip Art**.
- Save the page in your work folder but as well as giving the page a file name, click on the down arrow in the **Save as type** box and choose **Web Page** or **html**. Click **Save**.

File name:	This is my first web page
Save as type:	Web Page

- To see the page as a web page, open a **Web browser** .
- Click on the **File** menu and choose **Open**. Find the file in your work folder (left mouse click on **Browse**), double click on it, and click **OK** to see it in your browser.
- Keep the browser page open.
- Move between **Word** and the browser by using the bar at the bottom of the screen:

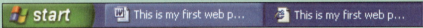

- Add and improve your page using **Word**. Click **Save** after each change.
- Each time you make a change, click on the web page and click **Refresh** to see the changes.

 Make a simple web page about yourself or a topic that interests you.

Design the page using **Word**. Add a picture and some text. Make changes to the text using the formatting tools – e.g. font, size and colour. Try adding an animated picture. Save the page as a web page and open it in the web browser. If you have some simple authoring software, browse the Internet for good ideas that you would like to try.

 Draw lines to match the clues to the answers.

- Use these tools to change text and layout.
- Software used to create websites.
- Language used to create web pages.
- Use this software to design a simple web page.
- Click this to update a web page.

Word | Html | Authoring software | Refresh | Formatting tools

Linking pages

Web pages are linked together by **hyperlinks**. Links are an important part of a web page.

They are used to take you from one page to another. You can also link pages of text using **hyperlinks**.

- Open **Word** and design a page using text and Clip Art. At the bottom of the page type: 'Go to Page 2'. Save it as 'Page 1' in your work folder. **Save as type: Word Document**.

- From the **File** menu, select **New** and design another page. At the bottom of this page type: 'Go to Page 1' and save it as 'Page 2' in your work folder.

- Open Page 1 again and highlight the text: 'Go to Page 2'.

- Click **Insert Hyperlink** on the toolbar.

- Open your work folder using the down arrow, highlight the file 'Page 2', click **OK** and **OK** and **Save** the page.

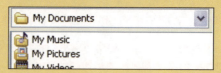

You have told the link on Page 1 to take you to Page 2 when you click on it. The words have now changed to a link: **Go to Page 2**.

- Open Page 2. Highlight the text: 'Go to Page 1'.

- Click **Insert Hyperlink** on the toolbar.

- Open your work folder, highlight the file 'Page 1', click **OK** and **Save** the page.

To try the links, open Page 1, click on the link: **Go to Page 2**. Use the link on Page 2 to go back to Page 1.

I Add **hyperlinks** to some pages to link them together.

a Make two **Word** pages. Type a question on the first page and an answer on the second and link them together with **hyperlinks**.

b Now try linking more than two pages:

Type ten questions on the first page and link each one to a new page with an answer; you need a different answer page for each question so you will need a total of ten answer pages. Put a hyperlink on each answer page back to the question page. Use the quiz to test your friends.

II Hyperlink search.

You used text to make a **hyperlink**.
Look at some web pages. What have they used to make a **hyperlink**? Find four different things.

a _____

b _____

c _____

d _____

Web favourites

Every web page has its own **URL**, a **Universal Resource Locator**. The **URL** is the web page's address. It appears in the address box when you visit a web page.

Address: www.google.co.uk

You can store the **URLs** of the websites and pages that you visit regularly in a special folder called **Bookmarks** or **Favourites**:

- Open your **web browser** and connect to the Internet.
- Type Address www.yahooligans.yahoo.com in the **address box** and press the **enter** key.
- When the web page has finished loading, open the **Favourites** menu and choose **Add Favourite**.
- Give the web page a name to remind you what's on the page and click **OK**.
- To open a page you have saved, connect to the Internet, open the **Favourites** menu, roll the cursor down the list and double click on the page you want.

I

Here are some websites to add to your **Favourites**. Use the **URLs** to open the websites – if you like them, add them to your **Favourites** list.

www.yahooligans.yahoo.com

www.citv.co.uk

www.lettsed.co.uk

www.ajkids.com

www.woodlands-junior.kent.sch.uk/coolchild.html

What name would you give to:

a ajkids? _____

b lettsed? _____

c citv? _____

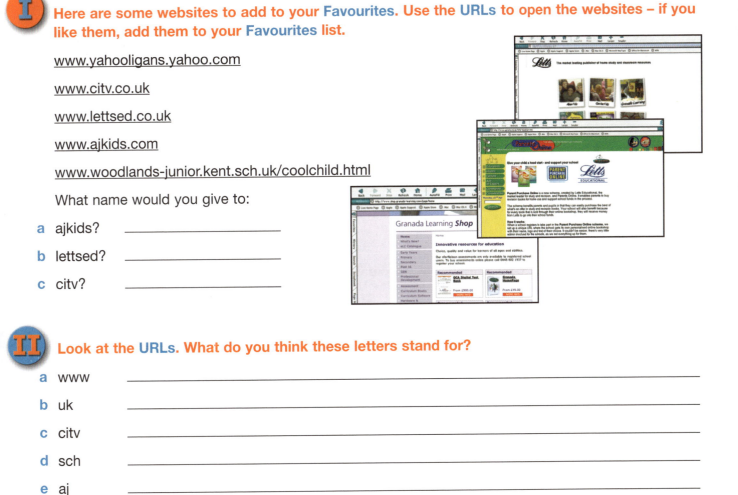

II

Look at the **URLs**. What do you think these letters stand for?

a www _____

b uk _____

c citv _____

d sch _____

e aj _____

f Look at the **URLs** again. What do you notice about the way they are written?

_____

Organising a Favourites list

As a Favourites list grows it needs organising.

- Open your **Internet browser** – there is no need to connect to the Internet to do this.
- Open the **Favourites** menu and select **Organise Favourites**.
- Click **Create Folder** and give the new folder a name.
- Highlight a saved page and click **Move to Folder**, choose the folder you want to move it to and click **OK**.
- Create and name folders for the pages you have saved. Click **Close** when you have finished moving pages into folders.

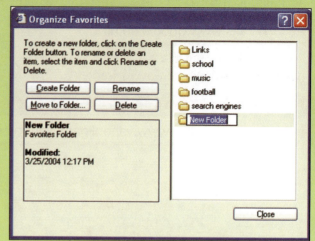

To open a page from a folder:

- Connect to the Internet and open the **web browser**.
- Open the **Favourites** menu, click on a folder to open it and click on the page you want to open.

To bookmark a new page and save it in a folder:

- Open the **Favourites** menu and choose **Add Favourite**.
- Click on a folder to open it and click **OK**.

 Create folders for the web pages listed in your **Favourites**.

Here are some suggestions:

📁 Schoolwork   📁 Fun and Games   📁 Search Engines   📁 Sport

Find at least two websites for each folder and add them as favourites.

 Here are some **URLs**. Check them out. Circle the folder you would put them in.

		Schoolwork	Fun and Games	Search Engines	Sport
a	www.yahooligans.yahoo.com	📁	📁	📁	📁
b	www.citv.co.uk	📁	📁	📁	📁
c	www.ajkids.com	📁	📁	📁	📁
d	www.thefa.com	📁	📁	📁	📁
e	www.iwm.org.uk/education	📁	📁	📁	📁
f	www.guardians.net/egypt/kids	📁	📁	📁	📁

Internet fun

Many websites use special software called **plug-ins**. These have to be downloaded onto your computer from the Internet. Your computer needs these so you can see and play games, or listen to music on interactive websites.

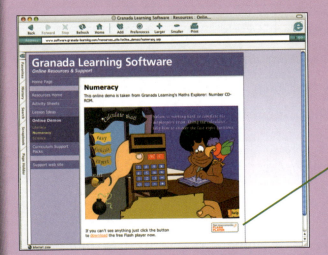

Popular plug-ins include **Macromedia Shockwave**, **Flash** and **RealPlayer**.

A good website has instructions on how to download the software from the web onto your computer.

A link on the web page will take you to the software plug-in page. From there you can download and install the plug-in.

Follow the instructions carefully and remember:

- Only download reliable plug-ins.
- Only download the free versions – there are versions that you have to pay for but the free versions will let you play simple games.
- Always ask a parent or adult before you download anything – some downloads may contain a computer virus.

 Visit these websites.

All of them need **plug-ins** to play the games, but they have links from their pages to reliable **plug-in** websites.

CITV
www.citv.co.uk

Yahooligans Games Site
www.yahooligans.yahoo.com/content/games

Black Cat Games
www.blackcatsoftware.com/tryme/

 Complete these sentences.

a **Plug-ins** are essential for some websites because _____.

b Popular **plug-ins** include _____.

c To load a **plug-in** onto a computer you have to _____.

d It is important to use reliable **plug-ins** because _____.

Surfing

To surf the web, you need to be able to use **search engines** and links.

Search engines are special websites that are used to find other websites. They search for **URLs** that match the key words typed into a **search box**.

```
flower AND parts    [Search]
```

1. The Great Plant Escape
www.urbanext.uiuc.edu/gpe/case4/c4facts1a.html

Hyperlinks take you from page to page when you are surfing the net.

To find and use a link, move the cursor across the screen until it changes to a hand shape and left click. If a link takes you to a website that doesn't exist any more, use to retrace your steps.

Here are some more **toolbar** buttons you will find useful:

Stop Searching
Use this if a page is taking too long to load.

Refresh
Use this to load a page again if there are any problems.

Home
Use this to go back to your **Home Page**.

History
Use this to see the web pages you have visited recently.

I Practise searching for information on the world wide web.

Go to

Use the **links** (not the **search box**) to:

a Find the capital city of Romania. _____

b List four categories of plants. _____

c Find the name of Orlando Bloom's first major film. _____

d Find the distance from the earth to the moon. _____

e Why and when did the gymnast Nadia Comaneci make Olympic history?
_____

II Answer these questions about buttons.

a Why is the **Home** or the **Back** button useful when you are surfing? _____

b How could the **History** button be useful? _____

c What could you try if a page didn't open when you typed the **URL** and pressed the **enter** key or clicked on **Go**? _____

d How can you find a **link** on a page? _____

e How do you make a **search** more accurate?
_____

Safety

Surfing the Internet is a lot of fun, but there are some dangers too.

A **chat room** is a website where you can swap messages with other people. Chat rooms are popular but to stay safe:

- Only use chat rooms or websites if they have been approved by your parents or a responsible adult.
- Use a nickname when chatting.
- Never give personal details such as your name, address, e-mail address, school or phone number.
- Never give any details about your family.
- Never arrange to meet someone from a chat room. Always tell an adult if you are invited to meet someone or if you read something that makes you feel uncomfortable.

A **virus** is a computer program that can send annoying messages to your screen or damage your files. Viruses can infect your computer through e-mail or computer downloads. Special virus software can stop some viruses entering your computer but to stay safe:

- If your computer detects an e-mail or a download with a virus – don't open it, delete it.
- If you receive an e-mail from someone you don't know, delete it.

Here are some fun websites to help you stay safe. Check them out.

Grid Club Cybercafe
www.gridclub.com/games/citizenship/cybercafe/base.htm

Internet Safety Advice
www.fkbko.co.uk

BT Safe Surf
www.btplc.com/ict/fun_stuff/safesurf

Make your own list of rules for Safe Surfing.

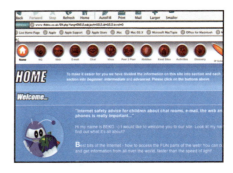

Which character or characters help you to surf through the pages on each of the three 'Safe Surfing' websites?

a Grid Club Cybercafe _____

b BT Safe Surf _____

c Who introduces you to the FKBKO website? _____

d List three things you could do to protect your computer against a computer virus.

_____

_____

_____

_____

Diagrams and charts

Use **diagrams** and **organisational charts** in project and science work to improve your presentation and to try out new ways of recording information.

- Open **Word**.
- Add the **Drawing** toolbar to the screen (**View** menu, **Toolbars** and click **Drawing**).
- Click on the **Diagram and Chart** button to open the **Diagram Gallery**.
- Select a diagram by highlighting the box and clicking **OK**.

Each diagram or chart has options for adding text.

When you open a diagram or chart you will see an **options box**:

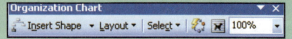

Use this to add extra boxes or shapes to your diagram.

 Create an organisational chart or diagram.

a Use one of the charts to show the life cycle of:
- A frog: (frogspawn, tadpole, frog).
- A butterfly: (egg, caterpillar, pupa, butterfly).

b Use a different chart to show a food pyramid. You will need four sections, starting at the base for carbohydrates, bread, cereals, rice and pasta. On the next level: fruit and vegetables. On the third level add dairy and meat products and then put sweets and fats at the top.

c Make a spider diagram with the title: 'The Victorians' at the centre.

 Use the menu boxes to answer these questions.

a How can you change the 'style' and colour of the chart?

___

b How can you add extra boxes or shapes to the chart?

___

c How can you delete a chart?

___

Word Art

Word Art is a useful and fun tool for creating headings and fancy text.

Open the **Drawing** toolbar using **View**, **Toolbars** and **Drawing**.

- Double click on  to open **Word Art** using the shortcut button on the **Drawing** toolbar.
- Click on a box to select a style and click **OK**.

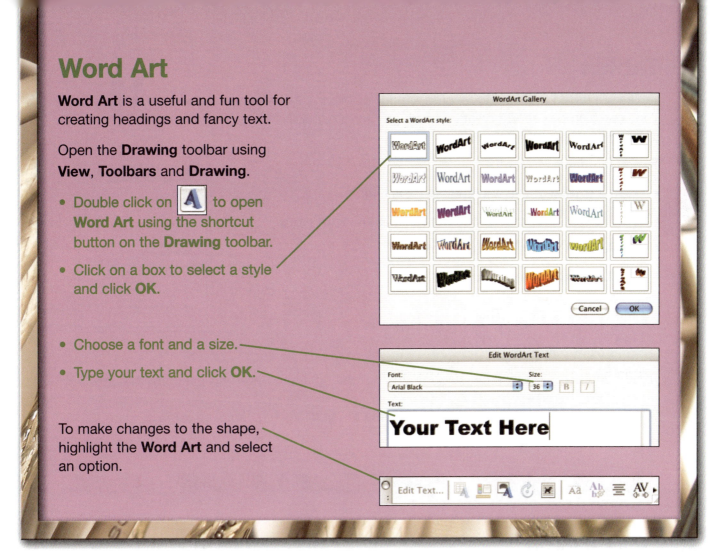

- Choose a font and a size.
- Type your text and click **OK**.

To make changes to the shape, highlight the **Word Art** and select an option.

I Use **Word Art** to create some colourful headings or labels for projects, posters and cards. Try these:

a The Egyptians
b My Bedroom – Enter at your own risk!
c Table Top Sale
d School News
e Happy Birthday!
f Playground Games – past and present
g Happy Mother's Day

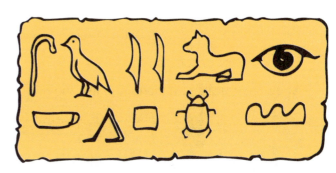

II Try the tools in the option box and then circle the right answer.

a lets you   change the size   change the font   change the colour.

b [icon] lets you   change the colour   change the shape   change the font.

c [icon] lets you   change the style   change the shape   change the font.

d [icon] lets you   change the font   change the colour   change the direction of the text.

Tables

Tables are useful for keeping records and for displaying the results of an experiment. They can also be used to create a blank grid for other activities such as crosswords, acrostic puzzles and wordsearches.

To create a table in **Word**:

- Open the **Table** menu and choose **Insert Table**.
- Type 4 in **Number of columns** and 2 in **Number of rows**.
- Tick **AutoFit to contents** and click **OK**.
- Type this text into the table:

Mon	Tue	Wed	Thur
21	20	22	21

To add another row, place the cursor in the bottom right hand box and press the **tab** key.

The **Border** tool changes how you see the gridlines – it can even remove them completely!

I Make a wordsearch.

Create a grid, ten columns by ten rows.

Add ten words (which can be between two and ten letters long) to the grid placing one letter only in a box. They can be arranged vertically, horizontally and diagonally, but keep a note of the words you add!

Fill the blank boxes with extra letters.

Use the **Border** tool to remove the gridlines.

Show the puzzle to a friend and ask them to use the highlighter tool to mark the words they find.

II Make a new grid with four columns and four rows and tick Fixed column width.

a Describe how the table looks on the page. How is it different from an **AutoFit** table?

___

b Highlight the cells in the top row and choose **Merge Cells** from the **table** menu. Describe what has happened. What could you use this for?

___

c Place the cursor on a vertical or horizontal line on the grid until you see this ⇔ or this ⇕. Hold the left mouse button and drag the mouse. What happens?

___

Making a booklet

Create brochures and booklets using templates and a template wizard.

To create a brochure using **Word**:

- Open the **File** menu and choose **New**.
- From the **Templates** list choose **Publications**, then **Brochure**.
- Follow the instructions on-screen for making the brochure's pages.
- Use everything you have learnt about word processing and desk top publishing to create the content for the brochure.

Here are some hints and tips as reminders:

To wrap text around graphics, double left mouse click on the graphic, click **Layout**, and click **Tight** or **Square**.

To move a graphic or a **text box**, highlight it, press and hold the left mouse button and drag the graphic to reposition it on the page.

To resize a graphic, highlight it, click on a corner handle and drag the graphic to make it bigger or smaller.

To place an object behind text, click the object, right click the mouse, click **Order** and click **Send Behind Text**.

To use fancy bullets, open the **Format** menu and choose **Bullets**. Click **Bulleted**, choose a style and click **OK**.

To remember what the toolbar buttons do, run the cursor across them and read the pop-up boxes.

I **Design a leaflet that provides information about your home area for people your age.**

You need a page for each of these: General information about the location; things to do; things to see; interesting facts.

Gather the information you want to include. Use the Internet to help you research the topic.

Plan your project on paper then use a template and create a booklet.

Add information and graphics to each page using WP and DTP tools.

Design a title page using **Word Art** and **Clip Art**.

Think carefully about your audience when choosing pictures and writing the text.

II **Look through the drop down menu boxes on the toolbar. Which menu would you use to:**

a Add page numbers? _____

b Arrange the text in columns? _____

c Use a **Thesaurus**? _____

d See a **Print Preview**? _____

e Use a **spell checker**? _____

Shop survey

Data in a database can be sorted alphabetically or by using a **Filter**.

Create a simple database using **Access**.
- Open **Access** and choose **Blank Database**.
- **Save As** 'SHOPS', in your work folder click **Create**.
- In the next box click **Open**.

Field Name	Data Type
shop name	Text
address	Text
postcode	Text
type of shop	Text
phone number	Text

- Add the **Field Names** and **Data Types** shown in the table.
- **Close** the box ❌, give your table the name 'SHOPS' and click **OK**.
- Click **No** to the next box.
- In the next box, double click on the table SHOPS to open it. Add records for five shops in your local area. **Save** the table.

To sort the records alphabetically, highlight a column and click  .

To find a particular shop:
- Open the **Records** menu, and click **Filter** and **Filter by Form**.
- Click the down arrow in the 'type of shop' column. Highlight the type of shop you want to find.
- Open the **Filter** menu and click **Apply Filter/Sort**.
- To show all the records again, open the **Records** menu, and click **Remove Filter/Sort**.

 I Create a database of 25 restaurants. Use these **field names**: Name, Type of restaurant, Postcode. Use the Yellow Pages to help you find information. Now answer these questions using **Filter by Form**.

a How many Italian restaurants are there? _____

b How many Chinese restaurants are there? _____

c How many Indian restaurants are there? _____

d Which area postcode has the largest number of restaurants? _____

 II Use this database to answer these questions.

a Name all the stores that sell food. _____

b Where would you go to have a photograph framed? _____

c Which shop could you contact on 1226972011? _____

d One shop is in a different area – which shop is it? How do you know? _____

shop name	address	postcode	type of shop	Phone number
Village Store	12 Main Street	S62 7TT	grocer and newsagent	1226450892
Little Gallery	76 Main Street	S62 7BW	picture framer	1226537629
J.W. Higgins	23 Church Lane	S62 7TY	butcher	1226348765
Merchant and Son	16 Hague Street	S62 5BR	grocer	1226388901
Johnsons	Retail Park	S56 1TT	supermarket	1226478222
Pots and Pans	16 Church Lane	S62 7TF	hardware	1226972011

SUM and AutoSum

A **spreadsheet** stores information as numbers, text or formulas, on a grid made up of individual cells. The cells are arranged in columns and rows.

Spreadsheets can carry out calculations using a formula.

A formula uses numbers and symbols and it always starts with an '=' sign.

- Open **Excel** and type the numbers in cells A1 to F1.

	A	B	C	D	E	F
1	68	101	59	90	119	345

- To add the numbers, place the cursor in G1 and type the formula =A1+B1+C1+D1+E1+F1 and press the **enter** key.

G
=A1+B1+C1+D1+E1+F1

- To simplify the formula use the word **SUM** and brackets: =SUM(A1:F1).

AutoSum Σ is a shortcut to use when adding numbers in rows or columns:

- Delete the formula in G1, click on Σ and press the **enter** key.

You should get the same answer as =SUM(A1:F1) – 782.

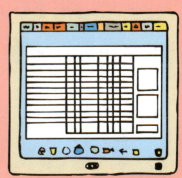

I

Use AutoSum to add these numbers. Type a and b in rows. Type c and d in columns.

a 37, 47, 92, 66, 24   _____

b 102, 213, 267, 354, 166   _____

c 2.5, 3.8, 4.2, 7.4, 8.1   _____

d 5.5, 8.7, 2.1, 10.6, 9.4   _____

II

Use these numbers to create a spreadsheet. Use the formula =SUM(A1:F1) in G1 and press the enter key.

	A	B	C	D	E	F	G
1	24	89	201	12	57	25	

Place the cursor in G1. What can you see in:

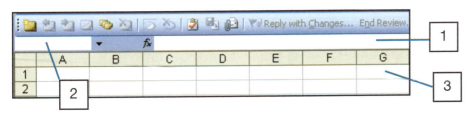

a _____

b _____

c _____

Copying formulas

Formulas can be copied from one cell to another.

- Open **Excel** and type the numbers 1 to 6 in column A.
- Type the number 8 in cells B1 to B6.
- Type =A1*B1 in C1 and press the **enter** key to multiply 1 by 8.

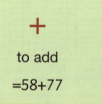

- Click on C1 and click **Copy** using the shortcut button on the toolbar.
- Highlight cells C2 to C6 and click **Paste** or press the **enter** key.

When a formula is copied to another cell, the spreadsheet program adjusts the formula to include the new variables and the different cell addresses then recalculates the answer in column C using the new numbers.

Use these symbols for the different number operations:

+	-	*	/
to add	to subtract	to multiply	to divide
=58+77	=10-7	=8*9	=20/4

I **Open Excel to create a table showing square numbers.**

Type the numbers 1 to 12 in cells A1 to A12. Highlight, then **Copy** and **Paste** them into cells B1 to B12.

Place the cursor in C1 and type the formula =A1*B1. Copy it to cells C2 to C12.

II **Look at the numbers on this spreadsheet.**

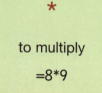

a   Which formula was used to get the answer in C1?

_____

b   Using the same formula, predict the answer for C2.

_____

c   Predict the answer for C7. _____

d   If the formula in C6 is changed to =A6/B6, what would the number be in C6? _____

e   If the formula in C4 is changed to =SUM(A4:B4), what would the number be in C4? _____

Changing variables

A spreadsheet automatically recalculates the answer in a cell containing a formula, when the variables used in the formula change.

- Open **Excel** and enter this data. In spreadsheet language, the length and breadth are variables because they can change.

- To find the area multiply the length (l) by the breadth (b). Type the formula =A2*B2 into C2 and press the **enter** key.

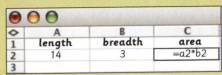

- The formula for the perimeter of the rectangle is 2x(l+b). Type this formula into D2 in the spreadsheet using =2*(A2+B2) and press the **enter** key.

- Change the variables (numbers) in A2 and B2 and press the **enter** key. The numbers in C2 and D2 change automatically.

The spreadsheet has used the formula to recalculate the area and the perimeter with the new numbers. This happens every time you change the variables.

I

Set up a spreadsheet to calculate the area and perimeter of these rectangles.

		Area	Perimeter
a	Length 19, breadth 15	_____	_____
b	Length 20, breadth 10	_____	_____
c	Length 16, breadth 12	_____	_____
d	Length 18, breadth 15	_____	_____
e	Length 25, breadth 21	_____	_____

II

The formula for the perimeter of a rectangle length 10, breadth 9, is shown here.

A	B	C	D	E
10	9	=2*(a1+b1)		

Think of another way of writing the formula to calculate the perimeter using the maths symbols + - * or /.

_____

Spreadsheet modelling

A spreadsheet helps you to solve mathematical problems or puzzles and answer 'What if...?' questions using numbers. It can also be used to check predictions.

A farmer needs to fence off part of a field. He has 24 metres of fencing to make a rectangular enclosure. He is not sure how long and wide to make it but he wants the maximum area possible inside the fence.

- Set up a spreadsheet with columns for length, breadth, perimeter and area.
- Type a formula for the perimeter in C2.

	A	B	C	D
1	length	breadth	perimeter	area
2	11	1	24	11

Using the mathematical formula $2 \times (l+b) = P$, the farmer calculates that $l+b = P \div 2$, so if the perimeter is 24, $l+b$ must always add up to 12.

- Enter numbers that add up to 12 in columns A and B, e.g. 11 and 1, 10 and 2, 9 and 3 and press the **enter** key.
- Copy the formula in C2 and paste it in cells C3 to C11.

The spreadsheet displays the perimeter for each set of variables in column C. The perimeter shown in column C should always equal 24, because the farmer is using 24 metres of fencing.

- Finally, calculate the area of each rectangle. Place the cursor in D2 and type =A2*B2. Copy the formula and paste it in cells D3 to D11.

I Open **Excel** and carry out two more investigations. In the first investigation the farmer uses 28 metres of fencing. He uses 20 metres in the second.

Enter the variables for:

a 28 metres. _____

b 20 metres. _____

II Look at the numbers in column D on all three spreadsheets.

Which shapes should the farmer use to get the maximum area possible for the enclosure if the perimeter is:

a 20 metres? _____

b 24 metres? _____

c 28 metres? _____

d What do you notice about all these shapes?

_____
_____

Graphs

Spreadsheets are used to create line and column graphs, bar and pie charts.

Graphs are created quickly and easily using **Chart Wizard** .

- Open **Excel**.
- In column A type the numbers 1 to 5.
- In B1 type =A1*A1 to calculate 1^2.
- Copy the formula in B1 and paste it into cells B2 to B5.
- In C1 type =2*A1 to calculate 2×1.
- Copy the formula in C1 and paste it into cells C2 to C5.
- Highlight the numbers and open **Chart Wizard**.
- Choose **Line Graph** and **Next**.
- Click **Series** and type x, x² or 2*x in the **Name** box to match the lines shown on the graph.
- Click **Next** and give the graph a title: 'Comparing Number Patterns'.
- Label the x and y axes: 'Numbers'. Click **Next** and **Finish**.

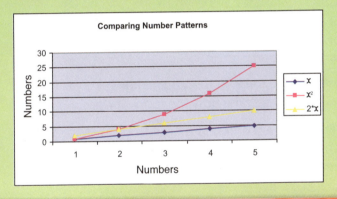

Practise using Chart Wizard to investigate number patterns.

Open **Excel** and copy the spreadsheet shown above.

Use the formulas given for columns B and C.

In column D1 type a formula for x + 3. For x substitute the numbers shown in column A. **Copy** and **paste** the formula in cells D2–D5.

Highlight all the numbers in the spreadsheet and use the **Chart Wizard** to draw a new graph.

Using graphs.

Change the variables in the spreadsheet: in A1 start with 3 and end with 7. Highlight the numbers and use **Chart Wizard**. Compare this with the graph for the first set of numbers.

a What do you notice? _____

b List three advantages of using a spreadsheet rather than paper to draw the graph?

_____

Loops and processes

Computers and microchips control equipment by using procedures. Procedures are clear instructions telling the equipment how to operate.

A computer responds to instructions received from input devices such as sensors and sends instructions to output devices such as lamps.

Lots of computer-controlled equipment uses input and output devices.

This flowchart shows how an input device sends a message to a computer-controlled system to turn a security light on or off.

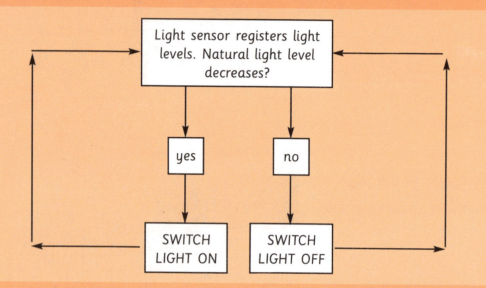

The process does not reach an end; it always loops back to the beginning.
Many processes have a continuous loop. The arrows show how the loop works.

You can use special software to set up a flow diagram and test a control procedure. The software allows you to amend and check predictions. When you do this you are carrying out a simulation. A simulation tests a hypothesis in an imaginary situation.

I Draw a flow diagram with text boxes and arrows to show what happens when a heat sensor (radiator thermostat) registers a rise in room temperature.

II Input or output? Circle the correct answer:

a Lamp: input   output.   d Light sensor: input   output.
b Buzzer: input   output.   e Motor: input   output.
c Thermostat: input   output.   f Heat sensor: input   output.

How does it work?

Many everyday devices rely on simple control procedures to make them operate. Sometimes, an output device needs two input devices to trigger an event. Sometimes one input device can trigger more than one output.

Many procedures also include a time delay.

Here is a control box. The box is linked to a computer and the following devices attached.

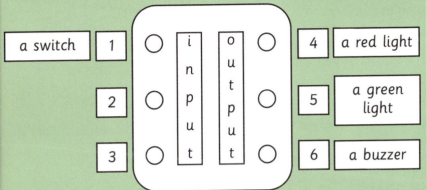

The computer sends the following instructions to the control box:

- when the switch is pressed, turn the red light off and the green light on.
- wait for 2 seconds.
- turn the buzzer on.
- wait for 4 seconds.
- turn the buzzer off.
- turn the green light off and the red light on.

In a very simple way, this simulates part of the procedure used at a pelican crossing. You could add extra instructions to make the green light flash off and on when the buzzer stops.

I What does a driver see at a pelican crossing? Colour in the flow diagram to show the sequence of lights that a driver sees when a pedestrian presses the button at a pelican crossing.

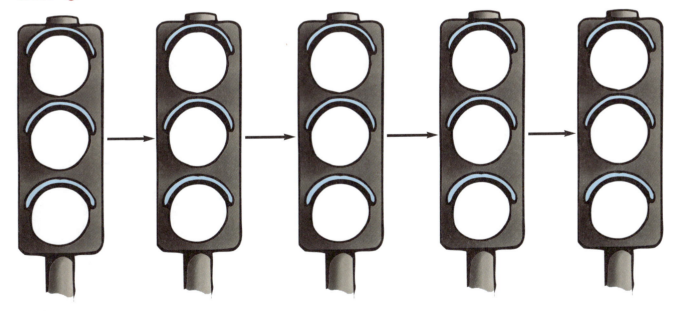

II Which of these does a ticket barrier use in a 'pay as you leave' car park? Circle the answers.

a Time delay   b Heat sensor   c Motor   d Switch   e Buzzer

Fun with Paint

Use **Paint** tools and a scanner to create some interesting visual effects. Save each draft so that you can see how your picture has developed or to go back a stage if you make a mistake.

- Choose a picture of a famous celebrity, a pop star or a footballer.
- Scan the picture into **Paint**.
- Save the picture as 'group 1'. **Save as type**: JPEG.
- Enlarge the canvas by dragging the corner.
- Highlight the picture. **Open** the **Edit** menu and use **Copy** and **Paste**. Reposition the pasted picture alongside the first.
- Use the **Paint** tools to add colour effects to the pasted picture. Use the magnifier to enlarge the image to see the small 'pixels' – the blocks that make up the image. Mix your own colour palette using the **Colours** menu and **Edit Colours**. Save as 'group 2'.
- **Copy** Picture 2 and paste it underneath Picture 1 to make a third picture.
- **Select** this picture using the select tool and click **Image** and **Invert Colours**. Save as 'group 3'.
- **Copy** Picture 3 and paste it underneath Picture 2 to make Picture 4.
- Use the **Paint** tools to add colour effects to Picture 4.
- Save as 'final group'.

I **Make a poster to practise using Paint tools.**

Scan a photo of yourself or a member of your family.

Design a group of four or six mini-pictures or make an even number of large pictures that you can print and mount as a giant poster. Use different effects for each copied image.

II **Use the tools in the Image menu and describe the effect each tool has on a picture.**

a **Skew** _____

b **Flip** _____

c **Rotate** _____

d **Stretch** _____

e **Invert Colours** _____

Making movies

Video clips can be used to create your own movie.

- Use a digital video camera to record some footage. Digital video takes up a lot of space on your computer so keep the clips quite short.
- When filming, keep the camera as steady as possible.
- Install the camera's software on your computer.
- Connect the camera to the computer and download the video clips. Save them in a pictures folder.
- Open **Windows Movie Maker**: click **Start**, open **Programs**, choose **Accessories** and **Movie Maker**.
- Open the **File** menu and click **Import**. Open a video clip saved in your folder. Keep adding clips until you have at least three listed in **My Collections**.
- Add a clip to your film by dragging it onto the **Storyboard/Timeline**.

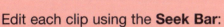

Toolbars. Monitor. My Collections. Seek Bar. Storyboard/Timeline showing order of clips.

Edit each clip using the **Seek Bar**:

- Highlight the clip so you can see it in the monitor and drag the slider underneath to the bit you want to keep. Open the **Clip** menu and choose **Set Start Trim Point**. Movie Maker removes any video before this point. Drag the slider to the place where you want to end trimming. Open the **Clip** menu and choose **Set End Trim Point**. Movie Maker removes any video from the clip after this point.

Join the clips, by clicking on one and dragging it so it slightly overlaps another and save your movie in your work folder.

 Make your own movie.

Plan a storyboard with four scenes and take some video to match your 'story'. Remember it only needs to last a few seconds. Here are a few ideas:

Making a cup of tea; My day; A visit to the shop; How to brush your teeth...

Use **Movie Maker** to edit your clips and add them to a **Movie Storyboard/Timeline**. Remember to save your work regularly. Click the **Play** button (under the monitor) to watch your film or show it through a data projector to see it on a big screen.

 How do you think you could make a title page?

Say which program you would use and how you would import it into **Movie Maker** and add it to your storyboard.

_____
_____
_____

ANSWERS

Page 2
I Check your child's answers.
II a The menu buttons stay the same on each page so you always know where to find them.
  b Search for sound clips or video clips using the search box or look for sound and video clip buttons on a page.
  c To make it easier to find information.
  d It takes you back to the Home Page if you get lost.

Page 3
II a anywhere on a slide
  b to add text
  c can be any size
  d slideshows
  e Use the Format menu – Slide Design or Background.

Page 4
II a Insert menu; Picture; Clip Art; File
  b Insert menu; Movies and Sounds; File; Movie Clip Organiser
  c SlideShow 🖥 ; the escape key
  d Movie Clip Organiser; world wide web

Page 5
II a digital   d Insert
  b download   e software
  c folder

Page 6
II Different versions of PowerPoint have different effects: you may not have all of these on your computer – but you may have others instead.
  a Object enters the slide from any direction and slides into position.
  b Object rotates.
  c Object picture builds up with the effect of a draughts or checkers board.
  d Object appears with a diamond shape in its centre which gradually disappears as the diamond shape moves inwards or builds up as the diamond shape moves outwards.
  e Highlight the effect in the numbered list and click on Remove.

Page 7
II All of them can be played on mouse click or automatically but these suggestions work best:
  a On mouse click so that instruments can be played in any order.
  b Automatically – messages usually have a start, middle and end so there is no need for a mouse click.
  c Automatically; this is better and less disruptive for young children who are watching.
  d On mouse click for a similar reason used in a.

Page 8
II a Fast forward and rewind.
  b Increase/decrease the volume; increase/decrease the speed; add echo; play backwards.

Page 9
II a You can see numbered mini versions of the slides.
  b It automatically changes on the slide.
  c Slides and Outline are used for planning storyboards and adding key text to slides. You can also use them to spell check the text or reorder the slides so they appear in a different slide order.

Page 10
II

n	s	p	o	n	i	p	s	p
a	n	i	m	a	t	i	o	n
e	o	c	o	l	c	l	u	i
d	e	t	v	v	e	c	n	t
i	d	u	i	i	f	l	d	x
l	i	r	n	e	f	l	y	e
s	v	e	g	w	e	x	e	t

Page 11
II CD's left to right link to: Formatting tools; Authoring software; Html; Word; Refresh.

Page 12
II Text, pictures, photos, buttons, animated gifs, diagrams, arrows (you may find some more!)

Page 13
II a world wide web
  b United Kingdom
  c Children's ITV
  d school
  e Ask Jeeves
  f There are no spaces between the words; and all the words are in lower case letters.

Page 14
II a Search Engines   d Sport
  b Fun and Games   e Schoolwork
  c Search Engines   f Schoolwork

Page 15
II a Plug-ins are essential for some websites because pictures and games will not run without them.
  b Popular plug-ins include RealPlayer, Macromedia Shockwave and Flash.
  c To load a plug-in onto a computer you have to use the link on the game website and follow the instructions for free download from the website.
  d It is important to use reliable plug-ins because viruses can attach themselves to a download; and they can harm a computer.

Page 16
I a Bucharest
  b Answers may vary but any of the following are correct: Angiosperms, aquatic, cacti and succulents, flowers, poisonous plants, seaweed, trees and weeds.
  c The Fellowship of the Ring.
  d 384,403 kilometres (238,857 miles)
  e In 1976 she was the first Olympic gymnast to score a perfect 10.